Seasons of the Moon
WINTER MOON

ALSO BY JEAN CRAIGHEAD GEORGE

Seasons of the Moon

WINTER MOON

JEAN CRAIGHEAD GEORGE

HARPERTROPHY®

AN IMPRINT OF HARPERCOLLINSPUBLISHERS

Harper Trophy® is a registered trademark
of HarperCollins Publishers Inc.

Library of Congress Cataloging-in-Publication Data
George, Jean Craighead, 1919-
    Winter moon / Jean Craighead George.
        p.   cm. — (Seasons of the moon ; v. 2)
    Works originally published from 1967 to 1969 in series: The Thirteen
moons.
    Includes bibliographical references.
    Contents: The moon of the winter bird — The moon of the moles —
The moon of the owls — The moon of the bears.
    Summary: A song sparrow, a mole, a bear, and an owl must struggle
through the cold, harsh months of winter.
    ISBN 0-06-442170-8 (pbk.)
    I. Birds—Juvenile literature. 2. Birds—Wintering—Juvenile literature.
3. Song sparrows—Wintering—Juvenile literature. 4. Moles (Animals)—
Juvenile literature. 5. Moles (Animals)—Kansas—Juvenile literature.
6. Owls—Juvenile literature. 7. Great horned owl—New York (State)—
Catskill Mountains—Juvenile literature. 8. Bears—Juvenile literature.
9. Black bear—Great Smoky Mountains (N.C. and Tenn.)—Juvenile
literature. [1. Winter. 2. Birds. 3. Animals.] I. Title.
QL795.B57 G384 2001   00-054231
598.8'87—dc21   CIP
                                                               AC

Book design by Andrea Simkowski
❖
First Harper Trophy edition, 2001
Visit us on the World Wide Web!
www.harperchildrens.com

CONTENTS

WHY IS THIS SERIES CALLED
SEASONS OF THE MOON?

Each year there are either thirteen full or thirteen new moons. This series is named in honor of the four seasons of the thirteen moons of the year.

Our culture, which bases its calendar year on sun-time, has no names for the thirteen moons. I have named the thirteen lunar months after thirteen North American animals. Primarily night prowlers, these animals, at a particular time of the year in a particular place, do wondrous things. The places are known to you, but the animal moon names are not because I made them up. So that you can place them on our sun calendar, I have identified them with the names of our months. When I ran out of these, I gave the thirteenth moon, the Moon of the Moles, the expandable name December–January.

Fortunately, the animals do not need calendars, for names or no names, sun-time, or moon-time, they follow their own inner clocks.

—JEAN CRAIGHEAD GEORGE

Seasons of the Moon

WINTER MOON

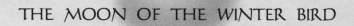

THE MOON OF THE WINTER BIRD

The half moon of December was obscured by a drizzling cloud layer that blanketed the Great Lakes states. The air was raw, cold, and growing colder. Beasts were in their dens, and birds were huddled on perches or in tree hollows. The longest night of the year was upon the land: December twenty-first.

This month was the moon of the winter bird. It is the month when the sun seems to stand still for several days at the winter solstice, December 21. On that day the Earth has carried the Northern Hemisphere as far away from the sun as it can go. As it starts back, all life seems to stand still like the sun, especially the winter bird.

On that evening of the solstice along the Olentangy River in Ohio, a blast of Arctic air turned the drizzle to ice. A row of glazed houses not far from the river glistened like holiday decorations in the glow of street-lights. One of the houses was yellow and almost square, the kind a child would draw. It creaked under the weight of the ice forming on its roof.

The house sat four hundred feet from the Olentangy River. Between it and the river lay an abandoned field where wild rye and sweet clover, goldenrod, teasel, and dandelions flourished in summer. Raspberry bushes and hawthorn trees speckled the field. Cotton-wood trees bordered it along the river. A meadow wilderness, the field lured children to pick wild strawberries in the spring and to chase butterflies in the summer.

Around the yellow house a generous lawn met the field in a carefree line of bushes: sumac, young maples, and alders. A toolshed and a bed of frost-blackened zinnias took up most of the side yard.

Close to the dining-room window grew a blue spruce tree. It was short, dense, and well pruned, and its limbs drooped as the drizzle on its needles turned to ice. A little sparrow, sleeping on a twig of the spruce, awoke. He cracked a frozen raindrop with his beak and moved two steps closer to the tree trunk. He went back to sleep.

He was a song sparrow, one of the most beautiful singers of America's fields and gardens. In spring and summer his voice explodes in bursts of trilling flute notes along roadsides, in yards, and in brushy fields. About two and a half inches high and gold-brown in color, he is not related to the house sparrows that hop on the city streets and nest in building cracks and eaves. The house sparrow came from Europe. The little songbird in the spruce was one of North America's thirty-four native sparrows. He and his kind spend their summers in thickets, meadows, field edges, and yards from southern Alaska across central Canada to Baja California, Mexico, and all across the United States from ocean to ocean. He is distinguished by his melodious song and the strong brown streaks on his sides and breast that converge into a sunburst on his chest.

The song sparrow should not have been in the spruce on this December night. Every other year he had been in Alabama with other song sparrows sleeping in bushes under warm, cloudless skies.

This year the Earth had not given him the message to leave. The declining daylight, which usually is one cue to migrate, did not set off his personal migration clock this year.

He had watched the departure of the one half of the Olentangy song sparrow population that migrates each fall. The other half stays in the north. His young had taken off into the wind, striking out for lands they knew only through inherited knowledge; then his mate had flown south. The catbirds, bobolinks, tanagers, vireos, and bluebirds had left. All had flown with deliberateness, following their own compasses down the continent.

Yet the song sparrow of the yellow house had stayed. October was warm, his food abundant; and although the short hours of daylight had told him to go, he did not. The time to migrate came and went. By November it was too late. The light was wrong. The song sparrow could not go.

He became a "winter bird." He would stay in the cold with those of us who live in the north. In our backyards and fields he keeps us company while he waits for the Earth to stop traveling away from the sun and swing back to spring.

The sparrow, like all birds, woke up in the night. At ten o'clock he opened his eyes. He could barely see, for he was a daytime bird, but tonight the gleaming ice around the streetlights caught his eye. Nervously he opened and closed his bill, as if trying to taste the meaning of the glitter.

His perch was the most sheltered spot on the tree. Out of the wind, it was warmed by the heat from the cellar window.

The drizzle stopped. The cold deepened. The spruce creaked and snapped under the heavy ice. The song sparrow dozed.

At six o'clock in the morning a buzz sounded above him. The alarm clock was ringing in the bedroom over his head. The light went on and the spruce tree sparkled. The song sparrow opened his eyes. Drowsily he listened, as he did every morning, to the ceremonial sounds of the people awakening. First came footfalls on the floor, then on the stairs. This was always followed by the clatter of pans in the kitchen. He had to wait a few minutes for the next noise, his cue to begin his day. Then it came. The door opened and the man of the house leaned down and picked up his morning paper. With that the song sparrow added to the droppings on the limb below him. The tidy pile told of the preciseness of his sleeping habits: that he slept every night in the same spot.

When the door closed, the song sparrow leaned down and peeked out into the yard through his "window" in the spruce twigs. He did this every morning in the winter, assessing the weather before deciding whether or not to get up. The Queen Anne's lace plants at the edge of the lawn were slick with ice. He puffed out his feathers and sat still.

The swatch of Queen Anne's lace was

important to him. It was the focal point of his daily activities. Three Februarys ago he had made his first trip north. Beyond Columbus, Ohio, he had looked down on a brushy fence row and recognized the field where he had been raised. He did not stop, however—young birds rarely return to their birthplaces. Nevertheless, the sight of his home slowed his flight. Ten miles farther north, he saw the broad swatch of last year's dry Queen Anne's lace. The seeds were a favorite food. He alighted on a dead flower head and looked around. He saw the yellow house, but primarily he saw the yard, the bushes, and the field. They were what he was seeking. They were song sparrow habitat. He scouted the area and then sat quietly.

As still as he was, a neighboring male song sparrow saw him. The neighbor flew at him, warning him to leave. The song sparrow was not intimidated. The patch of Queen Anne's lace and the yard were his. He faced his neighbor, who was perched on another dry flower head. Hunching low and puffing out his feathers menacingly, the neighbor assumed the "fight stance" of his species. Then they both flew at each other. They struck wings and beaks and, scolding, spiraled to the ground. The challenger hopped onto his wings and flew back to his own territory. The battle was over. The song sparrow of the Queen Anne's lace had won.

He flew back to the dry flower heads and burst into song. His bubbling notes informed the challenger and all his neighbors that this patch was his.

Immediately, he flew to the spruce by the house and declared his ownership of the tree with another burst of song. He went on to claim the rosebush by the gate. Speeding to the top of the toolshed, he announced that it too belonged to him. He then darted into the field and sang on a hackberry bush; however, the bush belonged to the neighbor, who instantly sped at him with raised feathers. The neighbor reclaimed the hackberry bush and burst into volleys of song. The song sparrow flew to a raspberry bush not far from this enemy. Both birds sang until they settled on a "fence" between the two bushes beyond which they would not go. They then went off to roost.

For days the song sparrow sang from the Queen Anne's lace, the rosebush, the toolshed, and the raspberry bush. He flew around and around his property singing, announcing to the other song sparrow males that he owned this rich acre of land. The song fences were as real to him and his neighbors as our wire and wooden fences are to us. The birds respected them and stayed on their own property.

Setting up fences was not all the song sparrow was doing. He was also advertising for a mate. The migrating females were on their way north, for very few were winter birds. One morning in March they arrived.

The older female birds found their last year's mates. The younger ones quietly looked for the male with the best piece of property. That meant land with many weeds for food, dense low bushes, and grass clumps for nesting sites. A good territory also had few predators such as foxes, snakes, cats, and the parasitic cowbirds.

Around noon, a female alighted in the rosebush. The song sparrow burst into song. She listened attentively. He flew around his property to show her how wealthy he was. He sang on the roof of the toolshed, on the dry stalk of Queen Anne's lace, and from the raspberry bush. The young female did not search farther. Instead, she preened her feathers. The song bird sang to her exuberantly from the Queen Anne's lace. When he was done, they broke seeds together. She pecked his beak. The song sparrow had found a mate.

Each year he had migrated south with his mate until this year, when he had turned into a winter bird. His life as a winter bird was good. Most of his neighbors were gone, and he was free to ignore fences and hunt over almost six acres of land. For the most part, he stayed on his own territory, where he knew the food sources and his enemies. This knowledge was his best defense against the cold. He only needed to fly over the toolshed to fill himself on beggar lice and dandelion seeds, or to drop into the cow parsnips for a meal. He knew where he could keep warm in folded clumps of leaves and where the house cat walked.

When the man of the house departed that icy morning and walked gingerly down the slippery path, the winter bird flitted to a higher branch in the tree and peeped out at the world. The street was glassy, the trees sparkled like crystal, and the air was cold. It chilled his bare feet. He pulled first one, then the other, into his warm breast feathers.

The morning was so bleak that the song sparrow stayed where he was. Automobile tires screamed as they spun on the ice. He flattened his feathers to his body in fear. No sooner had he done so than the damp cold penetrated to his skin. Quickly he puffed, creating dead-air spaces, the best insulation known to human, bird, or beast. Soon he was warm.

The back door of the yellow house opened, and the cat came out. She stepped on the ice, slipped, turned, and rushed back inside before the door could close. The song sparrow knew the cat well. Black with white paws and penetrating yellow eyes, she was a formidable predator. Even the weasel and the black snake could not strike with the silent accuracy of the cat.

To protect himself, he had learned where

she sunned and dozed. He had noted her pathways around his territory, and this knowledge had saved his mate.

Last April the song sparrow's mate had begun their nest in a clump of grass on the ground along the house cat's route. She had worked on it alone while the song sparrow stood guard. Usually he sang, but this time he clicked and scolded, warning her to leave. The warning only confused her. She worked harder, weaving grasses in and out of her nest and shaping it with her body for fifteen or twenty minutes each morning. She trilled as she worked. He clicked in distress. The morning the nest was finished, the cat walked down the trail. The song sparrow clicked, flicked his tail, and dove at the cat. The song sparrow's mate flew off and never returned to that site.

Because there were still no spring leaves to hide a nest in the bushes above the cat, the female began a new one under the dense, thorny raspberry bush where the cat did not walk. In three days she completed it. On the fourth day she lined it with fine grasses, and on the fifth day she laid an egg but did not incubate it. Each morning she would lay another egg until she had five; then she would settle down for ten days to incubate them.

After her first egg was laid, she joined the song sparrow in the fresh growing sprigs of Queen Anne's lace. They rested, then dropped to the footpath to bathe in the dust, for reasons known only to birds. While they were dusting, a female cowbird quietly stole through the raspberry bush and stepped down on the rim of their nest. The cowbird is a parasitic bird who lays her eggs in the nests of other birds and leaves them for the foster parents to raise. One of her favorite hosts is the song sparrow.

The cowbird jabbed the song sparrow's egg with her beak, flew off, and dropped it in the field. She returned to the empty nest and laid her own egg. Then she flew quickly off to hunt for other nests.

The female song sparrow returned to her nest the next morning to lay a second egg. She saw the cowbird egg, but because it was splotched and colored somewhat like her own, she ignored it. She laid another egg and joined her mate.

A few minutes later the cowbird took the second egg away and laid her own. The next day the song sparrow's mate laid her third egg. When she departed, the cowbird arrived to take the third egg. She alighted on a low limb and looked down at the nest. She did not see the stalking cat. The cat swung her paw, and the song sparrows were rid of their enemy. Not only do cowbirds pierce the song sparrows' eggs, but their young grow faster. They either push the smaller song sparrow babies out of the nest or starve them to death by reaching higher to get all the food.

The song sparrow's mate also saw the cat. With a cry of alarm she deserted the nest full of cowbird eggs. She built her third nest deep in the now leafy raspberry bush, where no enemy could find it.

By the end of June the song sparrow and his mate had raised two broods of five babies each. The song sparrow had helped to feed the young. Parent birds that look alike, such as song sparrows, blue jays, house wrens, and mourning doves, feed and tend their young. With parent birds such as cardinals, buntings, and robins, in which the males and females are markedly different, the females are in charge of building the nest, incubating, and rearing the young. Their males sing and guard the nest.

By the time the song sparrows' third brood was old enough to sun themselves and bathe— the last skills a young bird masters—it was August. The days were growing shorter, the internal clocks were ticking on toward October, and soon the winter bird would be alone.

On the day of the winter solstice, the winter bird, like the sun, seemed to be standing still. Long after he would have been up in the summer, he was still inactive. Two hours later he flew to the Queen Anne's lace, hovered over the icy surfaces, and flew on. He sped to the cow-parsnip patch. There under a dry leaf he found a dry twig to perch upon. Rumpled from the night, he began his morning preening. He took a feather in his bill and ran his beak down the shaft. The vanes opened and snapped back into place. Little barbs on the vanes locked with each other. He groomed his important flight feathers, then lifted each feather on his back and breast and aligned it with its neighbors. When he was done, he was not only streamlined for flight but insulated. The cold air could not penetrate his smooth cover. He looked down at his feet. A frozen droplet sparkled. He bit it, drank, and peered out from under the leaf.

The downy woodpecker, a resident bird that never migrates, was up. The bird called *pick, pick* from the elm tree, then, flying over the song sparrow, *yank*ed brightly. The sparrow flicked his tail but did not answer. The moon of December had stilled his voice. He watched the woodpecker.

The driller alighted on the maple and hopped straight up it, defying gravity as he listened for insect larvae. Suddenly, he hammered with such force, it seemed his skull would break. But he does not even get a headache. A heavy coil of cartilage between his beak and skull absorbs the terrible impact—like shock absorbers in a car.

The song sparrow did not see the woodpecker drilling, nor did he see the woodpecker fish out a larva with a tongue twice the length of his head. The song sparrow was looking at a stalk of wild rye and feeling hungry. Flitting to it, he ran his beak along the head until he came to a seed. He turned it on end, cracked it, and ate it. He topped this off with some dandelion seeds. The ice on the knotweed seeds was too thick to crack. His meal ended.

Hopping back under the cow-parsnip leaf, he fluffed his feathers and napped. Despite the cold the song sparrow was fatter in December than he had been all year. The snappy weather had increased his appetite, and with no nestlings to feed or song sparrow neighbors to fight, he had indulged himself in eating and taking fat-building naps. He was on hold, like the sun.

The woodpecker called again as he passed over the song sparrow. He was on his way to his hole in the apple tree by the gate. He did not like the icy weather and, having eaten, headed home. The woodpecker would climb down into his hole, where his body heat would soon raise the temperature inside the hole to a comfortable seventy degrees.

The song sparrow had no hole to keep him warm, and so he exercised. With quick wing strokes he flew to the toolshed, then to a fence post, where he rested. Below him a cottontail rabbit was licking the ice from between her toes. A meadow vole was tunneling under the icy weeds. Out on the street a man and a boy held hands as they inched along the glassy pavement.

The song sparrow flew back to the toolshed roof just as a flock of winter song sparrows came to the field. He joined them. Many pairs of eyes were better at finding food in these harsh conditions than one pair. They all darted over the wild rye and ragweed. He veered and wheeled with them, then dropped down on the zinnia bed.

At noon he left the birds and flew to the spruce tree. The needles on the tree squeaked in the cold.

After a brief nap he joined the chickadees in the thistle patch in the field. The ice did not bother the chickadees. They are drillers, often making holes in trees. Hanging upside down, they pecked the ice from the thistles. The seeds took off in the wind on their little parachutes. The song sparrow followed them to the ground and ate them.

In the afternoon a wind arose, knocking the ice on the trees and plants to the ground. A gray squirrel came down the elm tree, skidded over the ground, and dug up an acorn she had buried months ago. She stuffed it into her cheek and ran back to her leaf nest. The song sparrow flew to the Queen Anne's lace, now cleared of ice, and rested on a tough, old flower head before flying to the yard.

Late in the afternoon the temperature rose

above freezing. The rain returned. The song sparrow flew to his spruce tree. Sidling along his limb, he felt with his feet for that special spot, found it, and settled down.

The gate to the yard creaked, and the woman of the house came home carrying an armload of brightly colored Christmas packages. As she opened the door of the yellow house, the cat ran out. He skidded on the wet steps, turned, and ran back.

The sparrow yawned. The fringe of fibrisse—the bristlelike feathers growing at the base of his beak—trembled. These feathers are barometers of bird feelings. They stick out when the bird is agitated and fold back when it is calm. The song sparrow folded his fibrisse back.

Although it was still early, the temperature was dropping, and the winter bird was ready to retire. By bending his legs, he pulled a tendon that tightened his toes around the twig—now he would not fall in his sleep. The rain changed to snow.

Twilight descended. The wind howled. The streetlights came on. The man came home and stomped up the steps. As he opened the door, the song sparrow tucked his beak into the feathers on his back and went to sleep.

Around midnight the back door opened. The song sparrow awoke, as he did every night at this time. This was the cat's hour to hunt. She would prowl her pathways looking for mice and sleeping birds. The bird waited for her to come around the house, but she did not appear. She had skidded on the ice and was now yowling at the back door for the people to let her in.

The couple inside the house did not hear her over the wind, and eventually she stopped calling. Meowing in the cold, she sped along the side of the house to the cellar window beneath the spruce. The cat knew her property too. The windowsill was protected from the snow and wind by an overhang, and the windowpane was warmed by the heat in the house.

The song sparrow was alarmed. The cat was three feet below him, swinging her tail in anger.

The bird's fear protected him. Literally scared stiff, he could not move. Sitting still, he did not attract the attention of the cat, who relied on movement to see her prey. Although his feet grew cold, he did not pull them into his feathers. He did not scratch an itch. His life depended on his sitting absolutely still.

An hour passed. The snow piled on the needles and limbs around the song sparrow. Still the bird did not move.

When a wind arose and drifted the snow, the cat tucked her front paws under her chest and squinted. Not comfortable enough to sleep, she dozed with eyes half open.

Fear was using up the song sparrow's reserve of fat. By two in the morning he had lost considerable weight. He was growing alarmingly cold. Still, he dared not move.

Suddenly he was warm. The snow had piled up around him, holding in his body heat like a warm blanket.

Three o'clock came and went, then four. The cat dozed. The bird sat still.

Inside the house, the alarm clock went off. Footsteps shook the floor, then the stairs. Pans rattled. The song sparrow did not wait for the door to open. He defecated. The cat looked up, saw him, and leaped. But he was gone, a snowy rocket headed for the raspberry patch.

The door opened. The cat dashed through the snow, up the steps, and into the house. The man leaned down, but there was no paper. The plows had not cleared his road.

Smiling, he stretched and went back indoors.

Sinking into the powdery snow, the song sparrow panted in fear. His heart shook his entire body. Then he calmed down. Fear in birds is intense, but it does not last long. He flew to the dried ragweed stalks and ate his fill.

For the next several days while the sun seemed to stand still, the winter bird flitted and slept and ate.

On December 31, the moon of the winter bird was done. Another storm swirled in from the north. The woodpecker poked his head out of his hole and pulled it back in. The chickadees, roosting in the raspberry bush, did not get up. The squirrel rolled her head deeper into her belly fur and tail.

But into that wild cold morning flew the song sparrow. He was alert and bright. This day was eight minutes longer than on the day of the solstice. North America was spinning into the rays of the sun again, and the light was working its miracle. The winter bird was becoming a spring bird. A song was forming in his throat. He could not sing it out, but as December's moon went down behind the clouds, he cocked his head and listened toward the south.

THE MOON OF THE MOLES

In a cozy bedchamber under the earth, an Eastern mole was awakened by a violent tremor. She was no bigger than a child's hand. She lifted her cone-shaped and furless nose from her belly fur and instantly got to her four feet. The palms of her front feet, which are broader than they are long and tipped with strong claws, were turned outward for digging. But she did not dig. She ran. Alarmed by the shaking of the earth, the silvery-brown mole sped along one of her many tunnels in total darkness. As abruptly as the tremors had begun, they stopped. The mole breathed deeply and began to relax.

Above the earth, a full moon was circling the planet for the thirteenth time of the year. It was the moon of winter darkness in the Northern Hemisphere, the moon of the moles. For moles, darkness is life.

The little mole lived under a parcel of the Great Plains of North America—an expanse of flat land that lies like a belt down the middle of the continent from northern Canada to southern Texas. It slopes gently eastward from the Rocky Mountains for four hundred miles. In Canada the Great Plains include parts of Alberta and Saskatchewan. In the United States they include eastern Montana, Wyoming, Colorado, and New Mexico, parts of Oklahoma and Texas; and western North and South Dakota, Nebraska, and Kansas. The mole was two feet below the surface of the eastern edge of the plains near Crooked Creek, eleven miles from Montezuma, Kansas.

The Great Plains are semiarid. About twenty inches of rain a year falls on this land of grass, wind, and flatness. Trees, unless planted by humans, grow only in protected riverbeds. Once a territory of wild grasses where the buffalo and Native Americans thrived together, the great belt is now blocked off into farms and ranches. Wheat, milo, and corn are grown in the eastern plains. Cattle and sheep graze the plains of the west, intermingling with pronghorns, deer, and coyotes.

When the moon of December–January shone down on the Great Plains, the smaller mammals—the prairie dogs, voles, and ground squirrels—were in their earthen beds beneath the frost line. Some were hibernating until spring. Others were snoozing through the December–January darkness, awakening now and then to eat and stretch. The mole, however, was up and about, for she was as busy in winter as she was in summer, when the sun warmed her subterranean acre of Kansas.

The silvery mole did not relax long. The tremors over, and her fears conquered, she went to work. The frost had come far down into the ground during the night. Ice crystals crackled from the roof of her tunnel.

On the snowy ground above her, a coyote walked. A crow called to his mate, and a cottontail chewed on a raspberry bud. The mole did not know about these things, for she had never been out of the ground. Born in May in a nest of grass under a rancher's vegetable garden a mile away, she had become acquainted with plump radishes, but not their green tops. She knew tomato roots, but not their red fruits. Her world was underground. She was a digger, a member of the family Talpidae, who live under United States soil from coast to coast, and from southeastern Canada to the Gulf of Mexico. Seven species make up the family in North America, each differing from the others in accordance with the type of soil it lives in. The star-nosed mole likes damp meadows, moist woods, and bogs; the hairy-tailed mole seeks the well-drained soils of woodlands; and the mole of Montezuma, Kansas, *Scalopus aquaticus*, and her kin inhabit the loose soils of meadows, pastures, and open woodlands. The others like slightly different soils, but all live underground.

When she was a month old, the mole had left her mother and two brothers and had followed a family labyrinth to the end of the garden. With a bushel of dirt, she had closed the route back to her home, turned west, and excavated a tunnel far out under the wheat field. Her tunnel was neat and small, about one and a half inches wide and one inch high. After digging for several days, she had come to the rich loam along Crooked Creek. She smelled its many insects and worms and was pleased. Still unaware of the sun and the moon, she had begun her solitary life as an adult mole.

After settling down, she had carved a round chamber beneath a rock buried in the creek bank. She had filled it with rootlets and bits of root bark and woven them into a bed. Then she had excavated five runways from this central station until she had four miles of major tunnels. The Wheat-Root Run wound under the field. The Creek Run ran along the bank of Crooked Creek. The Cottonwood Run led in and around the roots of the cottonwood trees, and the Road Run went through soft loam and grass roots to the edge of the human-made country road. The Bridge Run, her favorite, tunneled off to a white-grub (beetle larva) community and on to the worm-filled soil near the bridge. These she relished, for she was an insectivore as well as a digger.

The mole ran her tunnels without seeing. Moles have lived in the ground for so long that their eyes have become functionless. The eyes are mere specks on either side of the mole's head, too small to register anything but light and dark. Skin grows over them. Many moles live their entire lives—one to three years—without experiencing more than a pale ray of light. Certainly this mole had not seen sunshine or moonshine, for she had dug deep.

Lack of sight did not bother the mole. She had inherited from her ancestors a highly developed sense of smell. She could "see," so to speak, with her nose.

As she ran along her tunnel this day, the scent of ice crystals in the ground speckled the darkness with chemical shapes. A worm appeared in the smelling part of her brain. She dug through the earth to it as if she could see it. She ate.

Her lightless "day" would last three hours; then she would sleep for five hours. A twenty-four-hour day on top of the earth was three mole days.

Although there is no night and day under the ground, just the times the mole is awake and asleep, there are seasons. The mole knew it was winter from the behavior of the roots. They do not die like the surface plants, they simply change their activities. The winter-wheat roots that had come down into the mole's tunnel soon after the crops were planted in September were no longer writhing as they do in the growing season, but were creeping and seeking. They were taking up minerals and water and holding them in their storage cells below the frost line. The roots were growing at their tips as they moved away from the cold. They were full and stiff with the food they had collected and stored for the spring revival of leaves. Fat roots meant winter to the mole.

The earth shook again. The mole sniffed, but could not "see" what was disturbing her world. Dirt fell into her tunnels, and a root, searching for soil and food, swung down and touched her nose. She nipped it flush with her ceiling and, nervous about the tremors again, paused to collect herself by brushing her fur. As soft as bird down, her mantle could be pushed backward, forward, sideways, or straight up. This kind of fur was necessary for her subterranean way of life. She could run forward in her tight tunnels, back up, or turn around without being made uncomfortable by rumpled fur. Mole fur has no wrong way to be brushed.

When she heard only silence for a while, she stopped grooming herself and left the rest of the brushing and combing to the walls of her tunnels. She was very hungry. Moles have to eat food in amounts equal to their body weight—an ounce and a half—each day.

Turning away from the tremor, she hurried along the Wheat-Root Run. Hardly had she gone a hundred feet when she came to a blocked tunnel to the outside world. She had made this while digging the run. When she had accumulated a large pile of dirt, she had dug a shaft to the surface. Then she had turned around and, passing the dirt under her belly to her hind feet, had kicked it up the shaft. The dirt had shot out onto the field above and piled up in a mound. Under the December–January moon, the mole mounds of soil from subterranean Kansas were still evident. Plants would flourish in them in spring, for moles not only aerate the soil, they also bring deep, rich loam to the surface.

The mole sniffed around her shaft—now blocked with loose dirt—smelled no food, and went down the Bridge Run, which was deeper and warmer. A few hundred feet later she came upon six large worms. They had begun to move downward around two in the morning, burrowed through the mole's ceiling, and fallen to her floor. She pounced upon them and ate with great relish.

She continued along the Bridge Run, stepping with her front feet and pushing with her hind feet. Her rear feet worked like pistons moving straight up and down. The narrow pelvis of the mole permits its hind legs to pump without interference from hips, a perfect design for someone living in a tunnel.

Her pistonlike stride gave the mole considerable speed. She moved swiftly, devouring every worm and beetle larva she came upon. After two hours of running and eating, she stopped at a boulder. It marked the end of her home range and the beginning of another mole's property—a male's. He had broken into her tunnel one day last autumn. She had been furious at him and had walled him off with a bushel of dirt. Today she did not feel so antagonistic toward him. February, the breeding season of the moles, was not far off. Without knowing why, she took down a portion of the barrier and listened for her neighbor. Then she turned around by folding her supple spine into a U and hurried back to her bedchamber. She rested briefly before taking off for the Road Run, looking for more food.

For several hours she dug and ate grubs, as well as a spider and a centipede. When her day was almost over, she squeezed through a particularly narrow, steep part of the Road Run to a patch of loose dirt. With her nimble feet she opened the door to another bed-chamber. This was an emergency retreat some six inches deeper than her central station, and therefore warmer. Arranging its root cuttings over and around her with her feet and nose, she sat on her haunches and tucked her nose into her tail. Almost instantly she was asleep. The mole's day was done.

Whatever the mole did, she did whole-heartedly. Now she slept with a vengeance. So deeply was she sleeping that she did not hear the next series of tremors down by Crooked Creek, made by humans driving stakes into the ground.

Five hours later she awoke and poked her pointed nose into her tunnel. She breathed deeply of the underground air. The air came from the spaces between the grains of soil, and was changed and renewed.

The fat nymph of a cicada appeared in the mole's nose-eyes. It was above her head, curled like a shrimp and chewing on the roots of a sunflower. She stood on her hind feet and dug it out of the ceiling, sniffed, and found another.

Feeling energetic now, she set out for the Creek Run. In a quarter of a mile she came to a cluster of buffalo-grass roots that marked the closed entrance to one of her summer tunnels. These runs lay so close to the surface, they were actually ridges above ground. In the vegetable garden where she had been born, the farmer trampled them and complained about moles.

Since this was the season of fat roots, the mole had no desire to work near the cold surface. She dug down.

In one minute she had gone six inches, found thirteen large earthworms, and eaten them all. Having consumed her ounce of food for the day, she went back to her winter bedchamber.

The next solar day on top of the earth began in the middle of the mole's night. A loud grating awoke her. Her body shook, the rootlets in her bedchamber shifted. She scraped back her nest material and, placing her feet lightly on the bare ground, listened through the circle of hairs around each palm. Through these she could hear—the mole has no external ears, just a ring of cartilage buried in the fur. Ears would be a hindrance to a creature that runs through narrow underground tunnels. Over the eons as the mole evolved, its ears had become useless and vanished. Sound-sensitive hairs had developed on its feet and on its short, almost bare tail.

The earth rumbled again. The rumbling came from close overhead. She sped to her most distant tunnel, the Cottonwood Run.

When her short-lived fear subsided, she slowed down to a waddle. The good smell of food was in the soil, and she dug.

As she worked, a hollowness sounded on the hairs around her palms. She was coming to a stranger's tunnel. She dug more carefully. It could belong to a mole-eating coyote or badger. With precision she carved the wall to cardboard thinness and listened with her palms. The new tunnel was small and narrow. Such a run could belong only to a pocket gopher or ground squirrel. These animals were friends, not enemies. With her nose, the mole broke open the tunnel and stepped in.

Her nose told her it belonged to a female thirteen-lined ground squirrel. It also told her the labyrinth was rich with worms that were feeding on leaf bits and grass blades brought into the gallery by this chipmunklike squirrel of the plains.

The colorful ground squirrel was fast asleep in her chamber at the end of a long tunnel. She had closed her door to the surface with grass and leaves in October and retreated into her labyrinth to sleep for weeks. Occasionally she awakened to eat, but not this day. The mole was free to investigate the ground squirrel's pantry of seeds. They came from sunflowers, clover, wheat, ragweed, bristle grass, and prickly-pear plants on the surface of the earth. All were strangers to the mole. She touched them with her palms, and an image of tiny underground river stones came to mind.

The mole took advantage of the squirrel's torpor and hurried through the squirrel's network of trails, eating the earthworms that had fallen into it and investigating her twenty-five feet of diggings. When the mole's three-hour day was over, she ran toward home. She could hear her nails click against the hard-packed soil of the ground squirrel's burrow.

As she arrived back at the hole where she had broken into the ground squirrel's runway, she smelled water. The squirrel's home was over a layer of gravel, an aquifer that held glacial water in the spaces between the stones. The water had been moving about a foot a year for ten thousand years. It ran slowly downhill through the vast gravel beds that lie in layers under the plains toward the Gulf of Mexico. Farmers and ranchers on the Great Plains dig wells down to this "ground water" and pump it to the surface for irrigation and drinking.

The smell of water made the mole thirsty. She scooped a hole in the gravel. The hole quickly filled with cool, clear water, and she sipped the refreshment. As her day came to an end, she sealed the break in the wall and scurried to her winter bedchamber. Buried in her rootlet snippings, she fell asleep.

The mole was awakened again by the earth tremors. She got up, put her feet on the floor of her tunnel, and, feeling the rumblings to the west, ran down her Road Run and north.

When she reached an iron fence post in the ground, she stopped and placed a front foot on it. It was her weather vane—it told her about the surface. The post was cold and shaking violently, not from the wind but from a great moving object that was hitting the post. She made a U-turn and headed off to her Creek Run.

In the rich loam by the creek she found many more earthworms but did not eat them.

She needed sleep more than food. Digging herself a makeshift bedchamber away from the noise, she curled up. The soil by the stream was a populated place during the moon of December–January. The mole dropped off to sleep listening to a moth pupa wiggle and a Japanese beetle larva chew.

She slept late the next mole day, then hunted her mile of Creek Run and checked for food in the Cottonwood Run. Among the roots she came upon a colony of ants. They were crossing her tunnel as they carried their larvae from the cold ground near the surface to their deepest nursery beneath a boulder. The descending frost was driving them downward. The mole ate a few larvae, then began a new tunnel at the end of her Cottonwood Run, far from the source of the earth tremors.

For the next two mole days she did not hear the rumblings. She relaxed, ran all her tunnels again, slept well, and ate heartily. She could not know that it was Sunday in the human world, and that the people who were making the earth shake were on their holiday.

That mole morning she smelled strawberry roots. Their odor carries far enough through the soil for these plants to stake out their territory with a strong scent. Other roots turn away from their chemicals and leave the soil to them. The mole found an active strawberry rootlet creeping into her tunnel. With a nip she ate its growing tip, on which hundreds of little hairs were clustered. These were the "mouths" that took in water and minerals. When the tip grew on beyond the mouths, they would vanish, and new ones would emerge around the new tip.

The strawberry root was a warning to the mole. The freeze was deepening. She made a U-turn and hurried to a musty layer of earth. It was made up of plant life that had once grown by the creek. As the vegetation decomposed, it became peat and gave off heat. The mole dug into this warm layer and made a Peat Run to protect herself against the cold and the noise.

The next mole day she broke into the winter home of a female bullfrog. The amphibian was hibernating—her front feet pulled up and under her chin, her back feet tucked under her cold belly. The frog's eyes were open, for she had no lids to close. A thin, transparent membrane protected them from dirt and grit. The mole kicked soil over the frog as she dug on, searching for grubs and worms.

That mole night she fell asleep listening with her feet to the crackle of a box elder's roots as they braced the tree against a lashing winter wind coming across the Great Plains.

Five hours later she scurried back to the Creek Run. Finding only a few worms, she dug furiously toward a gathering of white grubs

A little sparrow sleeping on a twig awakes.

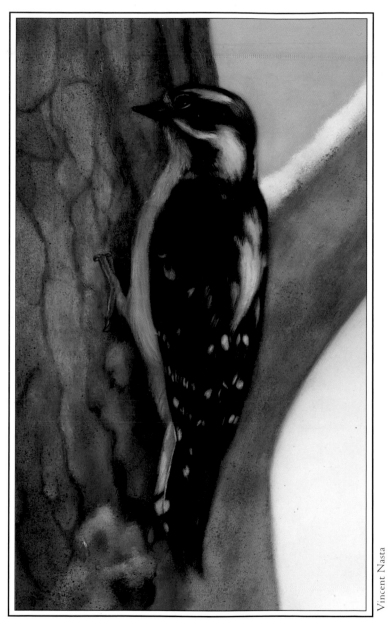

The downy woodpecker alights on a maple tree.

The mole kicks dirt
back up the tunnel to the field above.

The great horned owl stares into the moonlit woods.

A cottontail rabbit travels alone.

A doe lies under the ancient hemlock.

The bear sits by her den.

The raccoon leaps onto the hollow trunk.

and broke into the den of a pocket gopher. The gopher was awake and shifting her food from one pantry to another. She scolded the mole so ferociously that the little blind mole dug into the floor, flipped dirt on herself, and hid. The gopher screamed louder. Knowing that the mole would do her no harm, she then backed away and began moving supplies again.

The mole waited until the gopher ran off to a distant gallery. Then she uncovered herself, repaired the break in the gopher's wall, and ran a mile along the Bridge Run. Again the earth shook. The mole fled to her Cottonwood Run and as far down it as she could get.

The next day she began another tunnel off the Wheat-Root Run that would take her still farther away from the earth tremors. While she was kicking dirt up a shaft, she smelled a coyote. He was digging down toward her, snapping hungrily.

Terrified, the mole sprayed the coyote with

her protective scent, an acrid musk that burns the nose and eyes. The scent did no good. It was December–January; the gophers and ground squirrels were all underground. The coyote was terribly hungry. He dug on. The mole fled to the creek. The coyote heard her, pounced, and dug again. She ran the other way. He pounced and dug again, this time cutting her off from her runs. She would not live long without them. She needed the runs to provide enough food for her ferocious hunger.

She did not stop to think about that. She dug straight down, faster than the coyote could dig, then west, and with a snort broke into her Wheat-Root Run. She could run faster in her tunnel than the coyote could pounce and dig. In an instant she was in her main bedchamber. The coyote gave up when he could no longer smell her.

The next mole day the ground was quiet, and she was able to repair the Creek Run, which had collapsed under the tremors. She was working energetically—when suddenly she was on top of the earth. Her tunnel had been cut into and exposed.

The mole was terrified. No walls hugged her, no soil scents gave her a sense of direction. The air was loose and vast. She felt blindly for the hole she had just left but could not find it. Clinging to a stone that smelled of herself, she lifted her nose. The odor of steel and grease burned her nostrils. The smell went so high, she could not find its end. She was against the wheel of the huge machine that was cutting a swath for a superhighway across Kansas. The mole's loamy home by the river was threatened.

She stood very still. Animal scents blew up from the creek bed. A musky mink was fishing in the cold. A white-tailed deer was bedded down in the cottonwoods. A badger was digging for a gopher. From every direction came the smell of birds: pheasants in the wheat field, crows in the willows, juncos in the wind-break of the box elders.

Then she looked up. Her head glowed. Sparks crackled in her brain. The light from the full moon of December–January fell onto her tiny eyes, and the mole of Crooked Creek saw it.

For a long time she looked at the moon. Then a wind brought the scent of her own trail. She put her nose down and followed it. Within a few feet she smelled the sweet odor of her hole. She dove in, closed the machine-made rip with two bushels of dirt, and sat still.

As she did, a pleasant afterglow burned on her feeble retinas, and again she saw the moon of the moles, the thirteenth moon of the year, shining down on all the Earth's beautiful creatures.

THE MOON OF THE OWLS

The full moon of January rose into the stars. Its pale light shone down on the rolling Catskill Mountains in New York and turned the bare trees silver. A newly fallen snow glowed blue. The needles on a pine tree gleamed like glassy spears. They cast their pointed shadows on a great horned owl sitting on a limb against the trunk. He had just opened his large lemon-yellow eyes and was staring into the moonlit woods.

It was January, the moon of beginnings. From coast to coast, from Canada through Mexico, the great horned owl is the bold living symbol of this moon. Like the ancient Roman god Janus, for whom January is named, the great horned owl opens the door to all beginnings.

The owl, who stood almost two feet high, stared into the sunless forest. To him there was no darkness. The pale light from the moon and stars, and their reflections off the snow and clouds, fell onto mirrorlike cells on the retina of his eyes. The cells magnified the dim light, and he could see even though it was dark. He saw a snowflake on his great hooked beak. He saw a twig fall from the pine. Through these eyes, and his unique ears, the night is day.

The great horned owl is a magnificent bird of prey with tan and brown feathers, feet that are as big as baseballs, and heavy talons as sharp as darning needles. His wingspread is four feet from tip to tip.

He stood tall in the pine tree. He pulsated

the large patch of white feathers under his beak as he came awake in the roost tree. He had slept here almost every day for eight years. His reddish facial disc, rimmed with jet-black feathers, caught specks of starlight and directed them into his eyes. He lowered, then raised, the two earlike tufts on his head that gave him the name "cat owl." He was not trying to hear better, for his ears were lower on his head, but to look more like the stub of a tree.

The owl was large and grand, the winged tiger of the woods who, on this night, would throw open the door to spring. He blinked. No birds sang, no insects strummed. The frogs and toads were silent. It was a frigid January night in the Northern Hemisphere.

He circled his head almost completely around to his back as he surveyed his land. He did not see the woodchuck or the bear. The bats were either far to the south or hanging upside down in hollow trees and in caves. Their bodies would be cold, their hearts beating very slowly. They would breathe but twice in fifteen minutes. The season of hibernation was still upon the land.

And yet the forest was not still. The deer and foxes were walking in the moonlight. Mice were tunneling under the snow, and minks and weasels were sliding down riverbanks.

The owl lifted one of his flight feathers and ran his beak down the shaft to groom it. It snapped back into place without making a sound. Wisps of down grow along the edges of owl feathers and mute the rustling sound of their wings. When he flies, he travels as silently as a falling star.

The owl looked down on his six square miles of property in the Catskills, a combination of forest, fields, and swamps. On his western boundary rose a dark cliff. Over this landmark in autumn he and his much larger mate would chase their young of the year, sending them off to find their own homes, perhaps taking the place of a bird that had died. The old pair would also chase away other young of their kind who were looking for homes. They would not tolerate any other member of their species on their territory. It was to them food, shelter, and a nesting site for their young.

Suddenly the owl bobbed his head in excitement. This moon bespoke a dramatic beginning. He did not know why, but he wanted to be on the move this night. He opened his wings and flew.

He soared silently down the mountain, speeding between the tree limbs. Miraculously, he avoided every twig. He came to rest on a pine beside the "small-bird tree," where many of the daytime birds slept. The tree was an old beech with pale dry leaves that clung to it all winter. The little birds—cardinals, juncos, and finches—roosted among the leaves. Their body heat reflected off the leaves, making the space around each bird a warm little micro-climate.

The big owl did not see the birds, for they were sitting perfectly still. Then a cardinal pulled one cold foot up into his feathers and put the warmed one down. Because of that movement, the owl saw the little bird. He did not catch it. His food was bigger game: rabbits, squirrels, skunks, porcupines. For the most part he left the little birds and mice to the smaller owls, the saw-whet, who had come down from Canada for the winter, and the screech owl.

The great horned owl lifted his feathers and shook. He fluttered his white beard in excitement. Not because the pesky blue jay who screamed at him during the day was sleeping below him, not because the nuthatch had awakened in his tree hole and was leaning out to check the cold, and not because the sparrows and the juncos were striking their bodies with closed wings to keep themselves warm. He was responding to an exuberance within him.

He sailed off and, without making a sound, alighted on his favorite maple tree on the stream bank near an open field. He swung his head and glanced around. Nothing was moving, but he could hear tiny feet pattering. Now his eyes and ears worked together to pinpoint the sound with a three-point fix. The sound came from the empty crow's nest in the Scotch pine tree. The crows who chased and screamed at him during the day were roosting in a grove of pines ten miles away with hundreds of their kind. Yet the owl had seen their stick nest move. He focused his eyes acutely. A white-footed deer mouse who had taken up residence in the nest for the winter was getting up. The owl focused on the mouse with his fovea, an area of acute vision near the bottom of his eye. Another fovea at the top of his eye gave him acute vision in another direction. This dynamic winged tiger had keen vision up, down, and straight ahead, all at the same time. Although he was not above eating a white-footed deer mouse, the owl ignored the mouse. The call of his mission was greater than his hunger.

Bubbles moved under the ice in the stream below him. A mink was blowing air from his nose as he swam under the water. The bubbles flowed down his whiskers and over his back, turning his brown fur silver. He plunged over a sunken log and disappeared into darkness.

Presently he came up, slipped through a hole in the ice, and bounced ashore with a sunfish in his mouth. He put it down and shook his water-repellent guard hairs. Almost instantly they were dry.

The owl did not strike the mink. He knew

the animal was as powerful as himself. Curiously he turned his head upside down and watched the handsome mink in the top fovea of his eye, then righted his head and watched him in the lower fovea. The mink ate his fish and dove for another. The owl felt the night calling to him and looked toward his cliff.

Under the water the mink swam past the larva of a caddis fly. The wormlike animal lived inside a chimney he had built of tiny sand grains. The front door, a silken mat on a hinge, opened, and he leaned out and held his net of feathery mouth parts in the current. When he had collected several one-celled animals, he pulled himself inside, closed his door, and sorted the food from the silt. Then he opened his door and threw out the refuse, closed it once again, and ate.

A water spider under the stream sat inside an air-filled diving bell she had made with her silk and an empty snail shell. Here in her bubble of air in the warm water she would live through the snow and freezing temperatures that killed most land spiders. She was quiet, barely breathing. The mink swam past her, came ashore, and dived into the snow. He burst to the surface at the top of a rise, rolled, then slid downhill to his den. Well fed and well exercised, he entered his labyrinth through a hole under a rock and loped off to his bedroom among the roots of the forest plants.

The owl flew on with sudden urgency. He soared over an empty vireo nest and past the limb where the flycatcher sat in summer to wait for insects. The bird was in South America, but the limb was not deserted. Under the bark were the eggs of a cucujid beetle that had been deliberately laid beside the eggs of a bark beetle. The cucujids would hatch before the bark beetles and, as their mother had planned, the hatchlings would eat them. A few of the bark beetle eggs would survive, hatch, and burrow under the bark. The limb of the tree would die, and upon her return in May the flycatcher would eat both kinds of beetles as they matured and flew off.

The owl pumped his wings and climbed above the forest canopy, then soared down to a willow tree at the edge of his marsh. It was two o'clock—the coldest hour of the January moon.

He folded his wings and unfolded them high above his head. His white throat patch thumped. Energy surged through him, then died. He sat quietly.

Presently he noticed the beaver pond. Under the ice a beaver with an aspen log in his mouth was laboriously swimming, using his feet and steering with his tail. He emerged near his lodge and, bracing himself with his tail and feet, pulled the log with his teeth. He had cut it last summer and poked it into the mud to preserve it for the winter famine. Carefully he worked the end of the log up a watery tunnel and into his dry lodge. Here there was a room with reeds for a floor and mud and sticks for walls. His mate and his large son of the year helped pull the log into their home. They ate the bark only, gnawing and rotating the log as if it were an ear of corn.

When the owl could no longer see the beaver, he studied the marsh. A reed quivered, cracked, and fell. A muskrat emerged beside it. Muskrat was reliable owl food. Muskrats were active in spring, summer, winter, and autumn. The owl was contemplating taking the food when the surge of energy rushed through his body again, and he lifted and folded his wings.

He flew on to his oak tree above the marsh and the beaver pond, where he could see the cliff. He lifted himself into the air and dropped back onto the limb. January was speaking to him.

He took to his wings again, beating his way toward the cliff. He went over the rocky hillside where the black snakes slept. He did not see them, for they were under the logs and snow, wound around each other like threads in a ball of yarn.

The owl coasted over a hollow log where a mother skunk slept with her four youngsters of the past year. Skunks were a favorite great horned owl food despite the dousing of musk they gave off when caught. Nothing stirred at the skunk den.

He flew on, passing a porcupine curled up against the cold in a hollow tree. The porcupine instinctively knew that it was dangerous to sleep in a forest where great horned owls, gray foxes, Canada lynx, and eastern coyotes hunted. He had gone to sleep with his quills facing outward. An enemy would get a faceful of quills if it tried to pull him out. This had happened to one of the great horned owl's past mates, and she had not survived the relentless migration of the quills through her body.

Below the porcupine's tree a cluster of snow fleas was gathered. Their eyes glittered, but they did not move, for the air was too cold. They were waiting for daylight, when reflected heat from the sun would bounce off the snow and warm them. They would then thump their long slender legs and sail three feet into the air. When they fell back, they would thump and go up again. In this manner they danced the snow-flea courtship hop until the sun moved and they grew cold again.

Well past the porcupine and the snow fleas, the owl pressed harder on his wings and flew faster. He had seen a great horned owl, even larger than himself, skimming above the cliff. The other owl did not provoke him to chase, but to veer off to the pine grove and drop to his stick nest. It had once been a crow's nest, which he and his new mate of four years ago had taken over.

The owl picked up a stick in his beak. His throat quivered as the stick stirred memories of eggs and young. He lifted his wings and snapped his beak with a loud crack.

Flapping his wings, he shook off fine bits of fuzz from his feathers. He shook again. More fuzz floated away on the cold air. When he folded his wings to his body, he was more brilliant in color, more regal and spectacular. The moon of January was beginning the beginning.

A starling in an abandoned woodpecker hole scratched in his sleep and dislodged a feather. A brighter feather would grow in its place. The longer hours of daylight were bringing the plumage of the birds into breeding condition. Some, like the owl, sloughed off dull ends and became bright and vivid; others, like the starling, grew colorful new feathers.

The owl flew to the edge of a field. Something was moving. His keen eyes came into focus on the snow. It was the weasel. She was in her winter coat—all white, except her nose and black tail tip. She dove and leaped. She rolled on her back, flipped to her feet, and tunneled around a goldenrod stalk. She was not hunting on this night of the January full moon—she was playing. She was still a youngster from the past year.

A twig snapped and a red fox seemed to float into the field. His fur was loose and clean from the snow. He lifted his paw and bit the ice that had frozen between his toes. More comfortable now, he listened and stalked. Throwing his ears forward, he gracefully pounced on a covey of seven quail sleeping in a circle, heads out, to watch for danger. They burst out of the snow in all directions like fire bits from a sparkler. The agile fox walked away with one in his mouth.

A cottontail rabbit was bedded down in a cup of snow. She ran wildly before her enemy, the fox, and frightened a mouse, who skittered over the top of the snow. A screech owl plunged and caught the mouse. Then she flew back to the stub upon which she did all her hunting and eating. She swallowed the mouse whole. In the manner of all birds of prey, the great horned owl included, she would regurgitate a pellet of the indigestible fur and bones from her stomach sometime the next night before eating again.

The great horned owl shifted his gaze from the dramas below and watched the cliff. He looked away, then swung his head from side to side and bobbed it up and down excitedly. He had caught sight of the terrified rabbit as she flattened her ears to her head. Now she was still and the owl lost sight of her. By not moving, rabbits hide from their enemies.

The cottontail was alone, as were all the other members of her family. Over the ages they had evolved a system to protect themselves. By scattering, they made it more difficult for enemies to find them.

No longer seeing the rabbit, the owl flew on toward the cliff. He alighted on the top of one of the oldest trees in his territory, a whispering hemlock whose graceful needles cast shadows of lace on the snow.

Something moved near the tree's base. The owl dropped to a lower limb to see if this could be the source of his excitement, and looked into the large eyes of a white-tailed deer. She was standing alone. She was pregnant. Six and a half months from October, when she had mated, her fawn would be born. The baby would arrive when the tender spring leaves of the flowers and grasses were abundant.

The doe had been under the hemlock since sunset. All week she had browsed the dogwood and birch twigs with her herd in the valley, where they had gathered for the winter. Just before the sun had set, she had felt her fawn stir within her. Turning away from the herd, she had climbed the hill looking under every oak and beech tree along the way. At last she had come to the ancient hemlock. She butted its branches that reached to the ground and trampled the snow beneath it. Then she lay down. Limbs drooped around her; she could barely see the forest. Nothing, she sensed, could see her. She put her long slender nose on her shoulder and rested a moment. Then she got up and walked back to the herd. She had found a place to give birth to her fawn. She would come back to this place many times before it was born.

The owl preened his feathers. He strutted along the limb. The doe was gnawing the lichens on the side of a poplar tree. She pulled down the twigs of a beech tree and ate them.

Like the mice, the beaver, and the rabbits, the doe could find little green food in January.

Suddenly the winged tiger rose up off the limb and fell softly back. He pivoted and bowed. This dance had opened the door; the beginning was moving on.

"WHO WHOWHO, WHO WHO," he boomed. His white throat throbbed. His ear tufts sat straight up. "WHO WHOWHO, WHO WHO." His resonant voice was like a foghorn in the night.

"Who, whowho, who who." His mate answered from the cliff area, where she had wintered alone.

The owl spread his wings, flew over the treetops, the frozen waterfalls, the sleeping and active animals, and arrived at the cliff. He alighted beside his mate.

At dawn the Northern Hemisphere looked no different from the day before. And yet those haunting calls in the night had changed it all. The great horned owl had opened the door to the beginning of new life in the woods. The annual courtship of the great horned owls had begun.

THE MOON OF THE BEARS

In February the Appalachian Mountains from Canada to Georgia were rigid with winter's ice and snow. And yet the great stone and earthen mountain range seemed to breathe. It breathed in with the thaw of day and out with the freeze of night. The breathing moved the sap up trees in the warmth of the sunlight and down again by the chill of the moon. The thaw and the freeze split rocks and eroded chasms, and it brought hibernating creatures to consciousness and put them back to sleep again.

February is the moon of awakening and

sleeping, the moon of the bears. In their dens on mountainsides, in hollows, under logs, beside trees, they are coming slowly out of, and then sliding back into, their winter sleep. They are not alone in this. The plants and animals are all stirring and stopping under the moon of the bears.

A black bear was asleep in a shallow den under a fallen oak tree. The log lay in a Tennessee wilderness of hardwoods, conifers, and underbrush as dense as lawn grass. The hardwood trees were steel gray, their leafless twigs like icy webs. The limbs of the conifers— pine, hemlock, and spruce—drooped as if hugging themselves in the cold.

Around noon warm winds from the South blew into Tennessee, and the thaw began. The warmth remained for three days. A boulder near the bear snapped as the ice in its cracks let go. The snow began to melt and gurgle into the soil. The warmth reached the bear.

Her heartbeat quickened. Her breathing came faster. She opened her eyes.

Growling softly, she lifted her big, doglike head from her furry belly. Although she had not eaten since October, she still wore much of the thick layer of fat she had laid down in summer. It kept her perfectly warm in her icy saucer under the log. The leaves and sticks that covered her had sealed into a cocoon-like blanket by drifting snow. She matched the floor of the forest so well that not even the curious blue jays knew she was there.

The bear wheezed and lifted her head higher, further cracking her cocoon. She sniffed. Her eyesight was quite poor, but her nose was so keen she could smell the sap moving up the maples and birches and the scent of people three miles away. She could also smell delicious white grubs inside her three-foot-thick log.

She was one of more than a hundred

thousand black bears that live in dense woods near meadows and swamps of Florida; of the Appalachian and Rocky mountains; of California, Oregon, and Washington; and of Canada and Alaska to the Arctic Circle. Black bears like to live close to people, visiting towns to take hot dogs from grills or to walk through backyards and down highways. Black bears, unlike grizzlies, won't attack humans unless they are cornered or separated from their cubs by an ignorant person. They are not wilderness bears like the grizzly and polar bears, although they will live there. They prefer the woods near suburbia, farms, and orchards where their favorite foods abound. In recent years more and more black bears have been seen strolling in view of people as hunters put down their guns and pick up their cameras.

A black bear is also cinnamon brown, gray, creamy tan, silver-blue, and even white. The "white" black bear makes its home on Gribble

Island near British Columbia. All the differently colored black bears are one species, *Ursus americanus.* The grizzly bear, *Ursus arctos,* is three to four times bigger, less tolerant of humans, and nearly extinct in the lower forty-eight states.

As the sun went down, the snow melt snapped back into crystals, and the water stopped seeping into the soil. The freeze had returned. The bear slumped into a ball. Her heart rate slowed, and once more she slept. Gradually her breathing slowed down until she breathed only five times in two minutes. Bears are not true hibernators, for they can awaken if they must and go out to forage for food. On warm days in winter they sometimes get up and wander even if they're not hungry. For the most part, however, they sleep. They are semihibernators. The true hibernators cannot wake up until spring; their bodies become cold, their hearts barely beat, their breathing comes but once or twice a minute. Their awakening takes weeks and sometimes as long as a month. Among mammals the true hibernators include groundhogs, marmots, and some bats.

During the week after the first February thaw it became warm again. One morning the dripping and gurgling of the melt began before noon. The bear opened her eyes and cracked her cocoon wide open with her massive back and head. She rolled to her side and put her nose on the snow.

Two mourning doves were in a pine by the meadow. They had just returned from their winter home in Georgia and were quietly looking over their summer residence. It was at the edge of Tennessee's famous black bear country in the Smoky Mountains. Within the Appalachian mountain chain there is a steep ridge that runs from New York State to Alabama. All along the ridge the upland is speckled with inland swamps that the black bears seek for food, cover, and wallowing. The steep eastern front of the ridge is forested with bear staples: nut-bearing beech, hickory, and oak trees and fruit-bearing shrubs. At the bottom of the mountains are farms where apples and peaches fall to the ground. This is a favorite habitat of the black bears. They also live in the swampy and wooded areas of the East, the mountains of the West, and all across Canada and Alaska to the Arctic Circle. In these bountiful habitats black bears meet, fight, raise young, and stuff themselves on nuts and berries until their coats shine.

The warm thaw of February ended when a cold front arrived from the North. It sent the sap down the trees and put the bear back to sleep. She rolled into a ball and snored. She was three years old and five feet long from her nose to her two-inch tail. When she stood on all fours, she was more than two feet high at the shoulder. She weighed two hundred pounds. She was black as space and as rugged as a boulder.

Last summer she had been the companion of the big three-hundred pound male black bear, or boar, who dominated all the other bears in the area. He was a fighter. His face and flank were scarred from battle, and one tooth was broken. He reigned over thousands of acres of forest, field, and roadside—and other bears. He stood as high as a bicycle's handles, and he had a neck as thick as a basketball hoop. Last July the big boar had met the young female bear as he strode across a meadow of flowers and raspberries. A younger male bear fled as the boar came on woofing and snorting. Frightened, the young female turned and ran. The boar growled. She stopped and looked back at him. He woofed to say she should come with him. She did.

She followed him among evening primroses

into the night forest. She followed him along the top of the great ridge, then down a stream valley and into a campground. The boar signaled her to stop. She sat on her haunches. He walked past a tent where people were sleeping and, standing on his hind legs before a tall tree, reached up for a sweet-smelling ham. He could not reach it. It had been wired high to prevent just what the bear was attempting to do. This did not discourage the big bear. Climbing swiftly with fore and back feet, much like a lineman, he grabbed the ham in his teeth. With a twist of his powerful neck he tore it free. It was as if it had been hung by cobwebs, not metal wires. The two bears devoured part of the ham, chewing and snarling while the people slept. They did not eat it all, for the wind brought the delicious scent of elderberries, which they much preferred to ham. The boar carried the ham for some distance, then abandoned it by a stream.

It would be discovered the next day by crows and blue jays.

The next night the boar led the young female through dense hemlocks to a woodland meadow. There they ate cow parsnips and lilies. Although black bears will eat meat—a bit of a squirrel, an occasional mouse, frog, or snake—they primarily eat nuts, fruits, and berries. These foods create the mattress of fat they depend upon to get them through the foodless winter.

At dawn the wandering couple flopped down in a thicket and slept through the day.

On a warm summer night the boar came upon a wild bee tree. Rising to his hind feet, he pushed against it with his powerful forelegs. Three shoves and the old sycamore went down with a crash. Snarling and wheezing, he made splinters of the bee hollow with his teeth and claws. The enraged bees swarmed over him, stinging his nose, eyes, and ears to drive him off. The furry bear didn't even bother to swipe at them. He shredded the tree. The honey-combs spilled on the ground. Bouncing on the angry bees with his huge front paws, he woofed and wheezed until, defeated, they swarmed around their queen and departed. The two bears ate honey, bees, bees' eggs, larvae, and wax. When they had licked the last glob of honey from each other's shoulders and flanks, they rolled in the stream until their fur was clean. Their stomachs full, they went to their daytime bed in a hemlock grove. The day was hot, and they stretched out on their backs and snored.

During these summer days the bears became fast friends and then mates.

As the summer waned, the bears saw less and less of each other. One day in mid-August the big boar galloped up the mountain, pulled by the odor of ripening high bush blueberries on the ridge. The young female did not follow. She feasted on the jack-in-the-pulpit bulbs in the cool fern lands, wandered sunny fields, and swam back and forth across the stream to eat the berries on one side and the beech nuts and acorns on the other. By day she slept in a laurel grove beside a white cascade that roared over the edge of the ridge and plunged into the valley.

In the August moon of change she ate almost constantly, laying down the fat she would need for the winter. Even the late-autumn thunderstorms did not stop her from eating. As they rumbled over the Smoky Mountains and filled the valleys with lightning and thunder, she went on eating nuts and berries.

In late September the first frost gripped the mountain. White ice crystals formed where there had been dew the day before. The cold tripped a biological timer within the bear, and drowsiness overcame her. She shuffled off to a fallen oak she had found last summer.

Although some black bears just lie down under a bush or crawl into a cave or old groundhog den to sleep for the winter, the young bear scraped a saucer under the oak. The log was well hidden among laurel bushes and dense rhododendrons, birches, and hemlocks. Tangles of moosewood screened it from view.

The young bear made her den but did not go into it. She roamed the mountainside eating the abundant acorns at night and returned to sleep near the den by day.

The temperature dropped lower as the days shortened. The leaves stopped making green chlorophyll. As the chlorophyll faded, the red, yellow, orange, purple, and gold pigments in the leaves shone brightly. They painted the mountains with the festive colors of autumn. The birds departed for warmer climates, and the frogs and toads dug down into the mud and hibernated.

A snowstorm blew down on the mountain,

and the young bear became so sleepy that she stopped eating. Sitting on her haunches beside the log, she waited for the signal from the earth that would send her off to bed. Her head drooped, her chunky body rocked from side to side, and her big black feet curled up at the toes. She dozed and awoke, but she did not go into her den.

One morning in November the air pressed down heavily upon her. The barometer was falling. The sky was dark, the valleys plunged in clouds. The wind whistled along the ridge, bringing snow. The flakes fell faster and faster. The bear sat by her den. The snow melted on her warm nose and fur. Still she did not go to bed. The temperature dropped into the teens. A wild, blustery wind picked up the snow and drove it against trees and rocks. With that the bear got to her feet. Head down, eyes squinting, she walked to her den and went in. With sweeps of her paws she tossed leaves and sticks over herself, then slumped to her haunches. A bluebottle fly, too cold to move, fell from the underside of the log onto her fur and sat still. The wind and snow swirled on, covering the young bear's footprints so that there were no prints to tell where her den lay.

With sleepy movements she curled her head into her warm belly and put her front paws over her nose and her hind paws over her ears. With a sigh she closed her eyes. As the hours and days passed, she slipped off into the dark, faraway sleep of bear hibernation.

The signal that the bear had been waiting for was the storm. The frost and light snow-storms had made her sleepy, but it was the big storm that sent her to bed. It locked up the ridge of the Appalachians for the winter. All down the mountain chain where the storm had struck, the black bears went into their dens.

The young female did not feel the wind blow snow between the sticks and leaves she had pulled over herself. Time was standing still for the bear.

After the second thaw and freeze of February another thaw came to the mountain. The bear awoke and lay still with her eyes open. She twitched her nose to relieve an itch. The bluebottle fly had warmed up and was crawling along her big muzzle. It buzzed its wings. She shook her head. The cold air struck the bluebottle fly, and he dropped to her paw, too cold to move. She pulled her feet and head back into her den and dozed.

At noon the next day the bear felt moisture. The sap in the rhododendron was seeping out of a root she had cut open with her claws last autumn. In the noon thaw, the roots began taking up water and cell by cell, carrying it from the wet ground to the bear's den. It moistened the ground. Softly growling, she pushed a bough under herself and shoved her shoulders out into the woods.

She wheezed and breathed more rapidly.

Under the bark of her log a ground beetle moved its wings. They crackled as the insect walked down a labyrinth it had chewed last summer. It stopped at a spot where the bark had fallen off in the winter. Here the air was so cold the beetle's jointed legs could not move. He had no choice but to stay where he was.

In a warmer spot in the log a bombardier beetle became mobile and walked up to a many-legged centipede that had awakened a day ago. The centipede sensed the approach of this inventive but fearsome beetle. The centipede reared and opened its poison claws to attack—too late. With a pop the bombardier turned around and shot a bullet of boiling-hot formic acid at the centipede. It crumpled and withered.

A young queen wasp was awakened by the thaw. She moved her antennae and walked a few steps to investigate her home in the log. She did not go far. The sun had moved far down the sky, and the freeze was returning. In moments the wasp could not move.

The bear felt the freeze and pulled back into her den. The sun went down. The sap stopped running and slid back into the roots of the bushes and trees. Droplets of water froze, and the bear drifted back to sleep once more.

In the middle of the night she awoke. Murmuring to herself, she rolled from side to side, growled, and went back to sleep.

Before noon the next day she shuffled out of her den a few yards and stretched out on the snow. She smelled greenery. Digging with her two-inch-long foreclaws, she uncovered a chickweed. Her tongue rolled out, and she ate the lowly plant that was blooming under the leaves and ice. Near the chickweed the leaves of the hepatica were growing. The nubby heads of the wood violets were above the ground.

The early-blooming plants were racing toward the sunlight. The snow and the leaves were helping them grow. Like a greenhouse the snow held the heat from the decomposing leaves around the flowers.

The bluebottle fly felt the raw air and walked deeper into the bear's warm fur.

When the sun reached its apogee, the steel-gray tips of the hardwood trees glowed pink. The sap had reached them that day, and they were swelling and bringing the first color to the mountain range.

The sad cooing of a mourning dove floated down from the pine tree near the meadow. Presently the male alighted on a limb of the pine tree with a twig in his bill. His mate was looking at a stick she had placed on the limb. It wobbled and almost fell. The male put his twig beside it and both lay still. The doves touched beaks. A few more sticks and their nest would be ready for the two eggs the female would lay. The nest was not well constructed compared to other birds' nests, but it was still an inspiration to the male. At the sight of it he flew up in the air. His wings clacked as they struck each other above his back. He climbed one hundred feet above the nearby meadow and, on motionless wings, soared earthward. He sped downward in a sweeping arc, his wings held low. As he fell, the white on his tail glowed and his feathers clattered. Seconds before he landed beside his mate, he flapped his wings and slowed down. She cooed. He had flown the love dance of the mourning dove. Their eggs would be laid before the February moon had waned.

The bear awoke just enough to hear the crows caw as they flew in pairs through the trees. The moon of February had scattered their youngsters over the hills to find mates of their own. The old pair flew over their property.

Voices calling from the swamp crackled, *quong-ker-chie*. The male red-winged blackbirds were back from the south. The females would join them in a week or ten days. Four males arrived in the bear's swamp on this, the first wave of their spring migration. More would fly tomorrow. Then hundreds, thousands, and millions would fly up the Atlantic Flyway, the migration route of the birds on the East Coast. Some would stay in the Smoky Mountains, and millions would fan out to the North. A few of these would go on to the MacKenzie River in the Northwest Territories. An occasional pair would turn up in Alaska.

While the bear lolled on the snow, a chickadee sang half of his love song. A cardinal sang a brief part of his song. The moon of February is a time of awakening and slumbering for the birds as well as the bears. The longer hours of sunlight bring them into their bright breeding plumage and into song. On the days of the thaw they carol a few snatches of their territorial songs. These short beautiful arias are followed by long silences during the moon of the bears.

The temperature dropped below freezing, and the bear got slowly to her feet and walked back into her den. The bluebottle fly went with her.

Snow fell; the cold deepened. The sap did not run. The mourning doves sat on their limb and pulled their feet into their feathers. The chickadees hid in hollows. The bluebottle fly crawled into the bear's fur and held its wings close to its back. Life in the forests slowed. The winter was not over.

On the night of the waning quarter moon, westerly winds blew the storm to sea and cleared the sky. The stars and moon shone clearly. The bear snored. In a nearby sweet gum tree, a raccoon poked his head out of his doorway and sniffed. He pulled his head in. A few minutes later he looked out again and, clutching the tree trunk with his hind and front feet, walked to the ground headfirst. Gingerly he stepped onto the cold snow. He was restless tonight. Chuttering softly, he trekked off.

Nearing a sycamore tree, he smelled the scents of the home where he had been born and started up the tree. He never reached the old hollow. His father was leaning out of the hole, snarling and growling. The raccoon laid back his ears, jumped into the snow, and was gone.

He stopped in a grove of sassafras. The trees smelled pungent and clean. Suddenly another raccoon jumped on him. He reared to fight. It was a pert female raccoon. She ran around him, bit his ringed tail, and finally sat down and looked at him. With a chutter she got up and walked through the snow. He followed her over a boulder and down between tall spruce trees to an old hollow willow. She leaped to the trunk and, clinging there, sniffed down at him. He nipped her black heels. She dropped to the ground and jumped on him. She ran. He ran. She kicked up the snow. He kicked up the snow. Finally she galloped up the willow and climbed into her hollow. He followed her, for it was February, the time when raccoons pick mates.

Many nights later the raccoon came back from a fishing expedition. He climbed the willow as he had always done and started down the inside of the hollow to find the pert female. She snarled at him and bared her teeth. The mating of the raccoons was over. The little female would raise their offspring alone. They would be born in sixty-three days, when the crayfish and frogs were plentiful.

The raccoon backed up, scrambled down the tree, and returned to his own den. He went back to sleep. Like the bear, he had laid down a layer of fat that would keep him warm and sustain him until spring.

On the night of the last phase of the moon, the temperature dropped well below freezing. Nevertheless, the young bear woke up. Her heart beat steadily, and her breathing became normal.

With a rolling moan, and still half asleep, she felt her abdomen muscles tighten. She gave birth to a small, wet cub. She cleaned it lovingly until its black fur was dry and standing upright. Its eyes and ears were closed, and its back legs were limp. They would not develop into sturdy legs until it was time for the cub to walk safely out of the den and not get lost.

The cub was tiny, about as big as a person's hand, and weighed only eight ounces, the weight of a small jar of mustard. Blind, deaf, and feeble, it knew exactly what to do. It climbed up its mother's stomach to her mammae and nursed. While it snuggled in her warm black fur, she gave birth to another cub. When both were cuddled against her, she put her front paws around them, curled her head and chest over them, pulled her hind feet up over her head, and went back to sleep.

The moon of the bears had seen the birth of two beautiful cubs. They would suckle and sleep in their mother's arms until May, when the moon of rebirth was upon the land.

On a warm night in that month the young mother bear would lead two fuzzy, five-pound cubs out of the den into the woods. They would smell the new leaves, the busy insects, and the meadow beyond their den. They would investigate boulders and rhododendron bushes. They would tremble a little at the strange vastness of the mountain.

When they were comfortable with their surroundings, the handsome mother would walk slowly along the ridge and proudly show off her beautiful cubs to the wild community.

On that day the bluebottle fly would leave the bear den and fly to the stream. There she would lay eggs in the last bit of rotting ham, another reminder of last summer's events.

BIBLIOGRAPHY

Ahlstrom, Mark E. *The Black Bear.* Mankato, Minn.: Crestwood House, 1985.

Animal Kingdom: The Illustrated Encyclopedia. Vol. 5, page 26. Suffern, N.Y.: Danbury Press, 1972.

Bailey, Bernadine. *Wonders of the World of Bears.* New York: Dodd, Mead, 1981.

Bailey, Jill. *Discovering Shrews, Moles and Voles.* New York: Bookwright Press, 1989.

Brady, Irene. *Owlet, the Great Horned Owl.* Boston: Houghton Mifflin Company, 1974.

Burt, William Henry, and Richard Philip Grossenheider. *A Field Guide to the Mammals.* The Peterson Field Guide Series. Boston: Houghton Mifflin Company, 1976.

Buxton, Jane Heath. *Baby Bears and How They Grow.* Washington, D.C.: National Geographic Society, 1986.

Craighead, Frank and John. *Hawks in the Hand.* Boston: Houghton Mifflin Company, 1939.

Everett, Michael. *A Natural History of Owls.* London, New York: Hamlyn, 1977.

Forbush, Edward Howe. *A Natural History of American Birds of Eastern and Central North America.* Boston: Houghton Mifflin Company, 1955.

Ford, Barbara. *Black Bear: The Spirit of the Wilderness.* Boston: Houghton Mifflin Company, 1981.

Garelick, May. *About Owls.* New York: Four Winds, 1975.

Graham, Ada. *Bears in the Wild.* New York: Delacorte Press, 1987.

Hoke, Helen, and Valerie Pitt. *Owls.* New York: Watts, 1974.

Johnson, Fred. *The Big Bears.* Washington, D.C.: National Wildlife Federation, 1977.

Lavine, Sigmund A. *Wonders of the Owl World.* New York: Dodd, Mead, 1971.

McPhee, John. "A Textbook Place for Bears." *The New Yorker*, December 27, 1982, page 42.

Mellanby, Kenneth. *The Mole*. New York: Taplinger Publishing Co. Inc., 1977.

Moon, Cliff. *Bears in the Wild*. Hove, England: Wayland, 1985.

Morey, Walter. *Operation Blue Bear*. New York: Dutton, 1975.

National Geographic Society. *Field Guide to the Birds of North America*. Washington, D.C.: 1987.

Nice, Margaret Morse. *Studies in the Life History of the Song Sparrow*, Vols. I and II. New York: Dover Publications, Inc., 1937, 1943.

Pettingill, Olin Sewall, Jr. *Ornithology in Laboratory and Field*. Minneapolis, Minn.: Burgess Publishing Company, 1970.

Pringle, Laurence P. *Bearman: Exploring the World of Black Bears*. New York: Scribner, 1989.

Ripper, Charles L. *Moles and Shrews.* New York: William Morrow and Company, Inc., 1957.

Storms, Laura. *The Owl Book.* Minneapolis: Lerner Publications Co., 1983.

Walker, Lewis Wayne. *The Book of Owls.* New York: Knopf, 1974.

The World Book Encyclopedia. Vol. 13, page 575. Chicago: World Book, Inc., 1986.

INDEX

Alaska, 83, 86, 100
alder trees, 5
ants, 50
Appalachian Mountains, 80, 83, 85–86, 94
apple trees, 22
aquifers, 48
Arctic Circle, 83, 86

badgers, 46, 55
bark beetles, 67–68
bats, 60–61
beavers, 68–69, 77
beech trees, 62, 76, 86
bees, 89–90
beetles, 37, 42, 43, 52, 67–68, 96
beggar lice, 14
birch trees, 76, 82, 92
black bears
    appearance, 83–84
    feeding habits, 83, 86, 88, 89, 90
    habitat, 83, 86

blueberries, 90
bluebottle flies, 94, 95, 98, 101, 106
blue jays, 63, 82, 89
blue spruce trees, 5, 6, 8, 11, 24, 25
bombardier beetles, 96
box elder trees, 52, 56
bristle grass, 47
buffalo grass, 44
bullfrogs, 53

caddis flies, 66
California, 83
Canada, 80, 83, 84, 86
cardinals, 62–63, 100
cats, 13, 14, 15–17, 18, 19, 25, 26–28
centipedes, 43, 96
chickadees, 24, 29, 100, 101
chickweed, 97–98
cicadas, 44
clover, 47
conifers, 81